THE INDIVIDUAL AND WORLD NEED

Eberhard Arnold

PLOUGH PUBLISHING HOUSE
HUTTERIAN BRETHREN

Farmington, PA, USA
Robertsbridge, England

Edited and translated from the German by the
Hutterian Brethren
Farmington, PA 15437
USA

First Edition, 1938
Second Edition, 1993

Library of Congress Cataloging-in-Publication Data

Arnold, Eberhard, 1883-1935.
 [Der Einzelne und die Weltnot. English]
 The individual and world need / Eberhard Arnold.
      p.   cm.
 Translation of: Der Einzelne und die Weltnot.
 ISBN 0-87486-052-0
 1. Egoism—Religious aspects—Christianity.
2. Sociology, Christian. 3. Spirituality. I. Title.
BV4627.E36A7613 1992
233—dc20   92-30196
                                           CIP

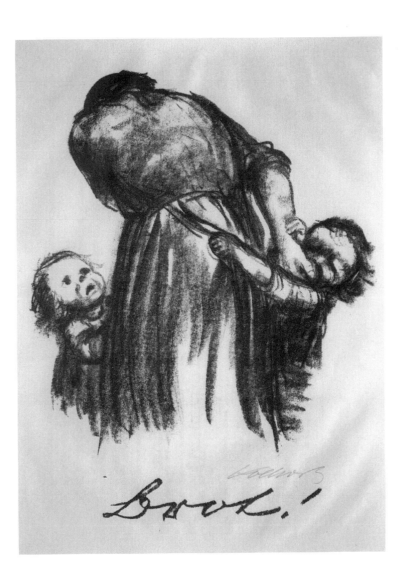

Brot!

The Individual and World Need is a translation of "Der Einzelne und die Weltnot," which appeared serially in *Die Wegwarte*, a periodical of the Eberhard Arnold Verlag, between October 1927 and February 1928.

PREFACE

It is depressing that so much of what Eberhard Arnold wrote is still valid now. His essential diagnosis of what is wrong in the world—fragmentation, alienation, lust for power, wealth, and possessions, the dominance of self-regarding emotions—all these represent a falling away from the whole, a falling away from God. The agony he has us confront is so grim, it could lead one to despair. But instead he faces despair head on, grapples it, and emerges writing about joy. How is this possible? Only because his faith is rooted in God and Christ. He sees God as love and community, as the expression of organic wholeness and dynamic, harmonious interaction—a theme he develops in the first part of his essay. It is his commitment to this faith that sustains him in the light of the horrors he describes.

What is important about Arnold's thinking is that he goes beyond the salvation of the individual. True, the individual is to be saved, though not as an egocentric individual, but as a member of the spiritual community which is the body of Christ.

Readers solely interested in personal salvation may not like this essay, because they have accommodated to the world and because they will not or cannot take Christ's teachings, especially the Sermon on the Mount, seriously. Like the rich young man, they cannot give up their attachments to the things of this world. Arnold calls for a commitment to the life of the Spirit which may seem too demanding. Yet without that commitment the world will remain as it is, full of illusions about self and material things and unable to see the consequences. The significance of what Arnold stands for is his faith that this state of affairs does not have to be. It can be transcended by the faith that moves mountains.

H. Otto Dahlke
Richmond, Virginia

INTRODUCTION

Eberhard Arnold's exhortation powerfully calls us to a whole new relationship with the poor, lest the credibility of our love for God be called into question. Although written in the 1920s, amid the pain and suffering of post-war Germany, it is a timely challenge to a world where millions claim the title "born again," yet where, at the same time, more and more of God's children sleep in street alleys, are enslaved to cocaine, are locked away in prison, grow up without a father, or struggle to survive in dangerously deteriorating inner-city ghettos.

To those of us seeking an answer to the overwhelming needs of our society today, Arnold's words strike a familiar chord. Our own church's story is a case in point. When the handful of whites and blacks who became the Voice of Calvary Church moved into our urban West Jackson neighborhood in the early 1970s, "for sale" signs marking the exodus of whites to the suburbs had already begun sprouting up. As blacks

moved in from nearby ghettos, it was very hard
to tell which whites were Christian and which
were not: all seemed equally determined to run,
taking with them the hope for trusting relationships across lines of color and class.

But soon even stable black families who were
no longer limited to segregated ghettos joined
the exodus. Once again, it was hard to pinpoint
the Christians. Anybody who could was moving
up and out, returning only for Sunday morn-
ing church. Left behind were those whom Jesus
called "the least of these"—people without op-
tions—the very people whose lives should be
touched by the Christians. The vacuum left by
the loss of faith and hope and leadership has
been filled with drugs, crime, broken families,
gangs, and poverty.

The growing gap between rich and poor in
our own community is found in hundreds of
other neglected places where Christians have
separated themselves from the pain of the world.

The challenge of this essay calls Christians to
the two thousand-year-old question asked of

Jesus: "Who is my neighbor?" His answer was the parable of the Samaritan (despised in Jewish eyes) who, unlike his "religious" counterparts, went out of his way to help a broken, hurting Jew. It was costly and inconvenient to leave his comfort for the sake of his enemy. We, too, in order to prove ourselves neighbor, must go out of our way to the darkest and most unlikely places in order to embrace the poor.

Jesus' call to be salt and light in places of pain and suffering turns us back to our own need for God. The weariness and disillusionment that inevitably accompany those whose lives are entwined with broken people creates, as Eberhard Arnold perceives, "real room for that real faith without which all hope is a hollow lie." Ultimately only the Church—the people of God—can possess that hope and faith. For God calls the Church to a whole other way of thinking and living in the same way that Jesus did. Jesus did not consider himself equal with God, but humbled himself and took the form of a servant (Phil. 2:6-7). He stripped himself of his rights and even went to death for the sake of human need.

It is because God has demonstrated his love to us that we are now to demonstrate our love for him by going into the uncomfortable, undesirable and sometimes dangerous territory of personal contact with the poor. It is through these relationships, black with white, rich with poor, that poverty takes on a face, race takes on the form of a friend, statistics become neighbors. In these deep friendships is the real hope for the salt and light of the Church among the poor.

Eberhard Arnold's challenge is a call for Christians to rise up, to show another way, to understand that the greater the risk we take, the more we forsake, the greater our service to God's kingdom. The extent to which we are willing to sacrifice is the extent to which we can be God's tools for healing among the poor. Following the example of the Good Samaritan will lead us into unlikely places and unlikely relationships—yet ones befitting citizens with enough faith and hope to give their allegiance

to an upside-down Kingdom. Eberhard Arnold
points us to a life that personally touches, and is
touched by, the lives of the poor.

> Spencer Perkins and Chris Rice
> Voice of Calvary Church
> Antioch Community
> Jackson, Mississippi

THE INDIVIDUAL AND WORLD NEED

EACH INDIVIDUAL HUMAN BEING is a living, coherent organism. All the organs in the body, and the individual cells composing them, invigorate and serve each other, giving and receiving life through the same blood stream. This is the secret of the animate body: its many diverse activities combine in one integrated whole. Each part of every organ contributes to the structure of the whole. Even the individual cells that make up these parts draw their life from ever smaller animate units.

The only difference between life's varied phases and cycles is their extent and their degree of intensity. The most living phase of this basic, primitive form of life is the time of growth, procreation, and birth. During these periods the character of life itself can most clearly be seen. The essence of life is expansion, movement, community, and reciprocity. Life consists in overcoming isolation through community.

This is true even in the simplest primitive cells we can observe in nature. Their life depends on their reciprocal relationship. Where is there a primitive cell that lives for itself? Does it divide only for its own sake? Its very division is a sign that it does not want to live alone, that it cannot live in isolation. It would rather make two living creatures of itself than go on living alone and isolated.

And when life has multiplied from this one-celled living creature by constant redivision into many tiny cells, here and there two individual cells mutually seek union. This new, reciprocal relationship of complete union results in new energy for division after division of countless little cells.

When we consider this continual sequence of division and reunion of the most primitive living cells, we could go so far as to see in it a developing system of life based on reciprocity. The constantly renewed relationships of so many thousand generations, increasing by division, show clearly how it would be if the entire animate world was like a steadily growing, living body. In the unified life of this body the simplest primitive cells would consist of the same vital substance as the whole. Recognition of their nature would be crucial to an understanding of life itself. This ocean of dividing and fecund cells flooding over and pouring through the entire earth would, one might conclude, be drawn together by a common consciousness, a unifying spirit, into one living unit.

The development of life on this earth, however, has not kept to that course. The individual, primal forms of life have not filled every part of creation with their simple life, nor coursed like a bloodstream through all the earth as through a steadily growing, united structure.

Creation has taken a different path. It has progressed to ever more delicate, complex, and differentiated forms of life and is now striving to unite these extremely varied forms into a unified whole. So today we find manifold variety in the animate world. At the first glance we can clearly distinguish between the physical forms of plants, animals, and human beings.

Yet even in this composite structure with its wealth of varied organisms, in the abundance of these animate bodies, the secret of life is repeatedly revealed: no living creature wants to be alone. At all times and all places life consists in individuals serving one another and building creative, living relationships. Life is community. There is no other life.

Regarding all these different physical forms—especially our own extremely complex organism—we may well be tempted to ask: how can the stomachs inside our bodies, the ears at work in our heads, and all the other organs that live and function inside us—how can they be brought to a consciousness of unity? Couldn't we consider stomach and lungs as separate animate beings assembled inside the human body only for a limited sort of common interest? Are they not separate creatures, simple or complex, which cooperate physically with others such as the muscles of the heart and the eyes just for their own limited ends?

But then we go from one puzzle to another as we ponder how any consciousness of unity can prevail in such a complicated body. Perhaps there lies hidden within us a subconscious awareness in the stomach that is concerned only with eating, drinking, and digestion and is far more independent of our general consciousness than our general consciousness is of the stomach with its hunger pangs or feelings of repletion? To grasp all this is impossible. All we know is that no matter how complex the processes within the various organs may be, the body has vital energy and capacity to function because they are linked by one pervading consciousness into one unified organism.

EVEN A BABY, at an age difficult for us to identify with, begins to sense his own unity of consciousness, though of course, he does it differently from us adults. He feels that not only the parts of his own person but also everything he sees, everything happening to him, belongs to his consciousness as a whole. A baby is unable to regard his body as the boundary of his existence. He sees farther than we do. The toy hanging over his carriage appears to him just as much a part of his life as the finger he moves or the big toes he puts into his mouth. Subconsciously he lives with a unified awareness of all he perceives through his senses and experience. There is unity about all that enters his consciousness.

Later he begins to draw distinctions. The child now begins to speak of himself in the third person. "He" wants the bottle, or "she" wants some other thing. Later still the child's growing realization of himself as an individual emerges as consciousness of his own ego. The child speaks of himself as "I," strongly emphasizing the demands of this "I"—as claims made for the little person himself.

In this period, with its extreme of "healthy egoism," the child wants to assert himself as "I" before he is able to go on to the greater "we" of community. Once he has attained—slowly and reluctantly—to the concept of the individual self and its limitations, community and the greater "we" that includes people and animals is once again sought and found.

The true child, however, is aware of a mystery above and behind these that is the fulfillment of all he has sensed must exist: the great "Thou" of God with his stars, angels, and spirits. A child has the closest and most living relationship to God, from whom, from the point of view of a tiny infant, he did not at first seem separate in any way.

We grown-ups too quickly forget this process of isolation. In a surprising way we reach a point where each individual feels himself to be quite separate: a particular, entirely independent unit of consciousness. If we are honest, we find it perplexing that there are other conscious units besides our own ego. As long as we remain in this egocentric state—recognized afterward as a bitter and inevitable malady of life—it amazes us that other people make the same exaggerated

claims to self-importance as we feel entitled to
do. As "healthy egoists" all men are completely
taken up with their own small selves, both in
their secret thoughts and, above all, in their basic attitude to life. They go as far as Max Stirner
in his book *The Individual and His Property*. He
writes frankly:

> My dealings with the world—what is their
> purpose? I want to enjoy the world; there-
> fore it must be mine. All I want is to have
> power over the world. I want to make it my
> property; that is, I want to be able to enjoy
> it. I take advantage of the world and the
> people in it. My enjoyment and my happi-
> ness consist in refreshing myself at the cost
> of their happiness and their enjoyment.
> But as for me, I never sacrifice myself; I
> remain an egotist and relish it! I am not
> one ego among others: I am the sole ego. I
> am unique.

No one should imagine that he is far re-
moved from this extreme egotism and its will to

possess. Each one of us needs to ask himself whether in his "private" life or as self-centered representative of his family, nation, race, or class, he does not in fact live as Max Stirner describes:

> I exist only for myself. Everything I see and enjoy, everything I take in hand and carry out, is all for myself. Whether I love a person in order to enjoy him, or whether I hate a person in order to eliminate him, I do it to expand and protect my sphere of influence. Either I am "good" to the "loved" person because it enables me to take pleasure in him and because I need a larger support group to help me assert myself and increase my power—or I wrong those who might hinder, disturb, or restrain me, who stand in the way of my enjoying life. I live for myself and my power alone, for myself and for nothing else.

The history of philosophy, especially in the West, shows us where conscious thoughts lead when this course is pursued daily and when—though in fact this seldom occurs—all one's thinking consistently starts and ends with oneself. The philosophic egotist, believing he is the only source for his thoughts, cannot help but tell himself: "I certainly see people talking, and I see others listening and acting, but it all has no objective existence. It exists only in my consciousness. I believe in only one thing—my own existence."

There have been thinkers, for example, who have laid an empty book on the table and asked themselves what they could enter in this book as perfectly certain, as something which they would be absolutely sure about. One of these philosophers wrote his logical conclusion on the first page: "I think, therefore I am. I am, since I have a consciousness."

And it is surely the most remarkable step in the whole progression, that still more radical doubters have had to cross out this proposition as well. They have lost even the certainty that they themselves exist, and since this last rational doubt puts in question the one subject that the isolated individual thinks about—his own small ego—it leads to an inkling of an "epistemological subject." In the end, it leads to belief in the all-embracing consciousness of the only great "I"—to faith in God.

Most people, however, who concentrate on their own selves hold on to the assurance, "I am, because I am conscious. I am, for I can think." All I need for my thinking and existence is my own ego.

SO BY LOGICAL DEDUCTION some people actually reach a state in which the isolating of the self brings total disregard or even denial of the existence of other living beings. When those who probe deepest are forced to invalidate their own personal existence as well, and even to dismiss the possibility of any objective existence, it becomes obvious what a morbid, death-ridden state they are in. For more constructive thinkers however, consciousness itself demands that they recognize this state as a mortally diseased condition. In positive response to this demand, healing begins immediately; consciousness recognizes its true nature and origin in the greatest of all selves [the "I am"], where there is no longer any isolation, in the vibrant unity of life. It can then perceive the source and context of life and the thoughts and actions these entail. Just as the little child's awareness goes beyond the bounds of his own small body, so in the life of a person with widely ranging thoughts, it reaches out infinitely far, beyond anything an individual's physical and mental powers can achieve. Basically, consciousness is all-embracing consciousness; its cosmic outlook goes beyond the bounds of the whole world, as well as deep into its depths. Ultimately, it is consciousness of the divine.

Consciousness wants to comprehend everything, to penetrate everything. It cannot remain content with what I am as an individual and what I do within the limits of my individuality. Consciousness both demands of me and impels me to measure and to penetrate the breadth and depth of the earth and of the entire stellar system. Consciousness demands what for me is impossible: to survey the whole history of life and of the spirit, and to perceive the deep coherent relationship of the whole.

Consciousness demands that mind and spirit strive for what is infinite. It demands totality and universality; it demands the whole, the comprehension and penetration of the whole of life. This is how consciousness proves it is alive. It is bound to be hostile to isolation in every form.

Our conscious spirit, its longing for infinity, points to our source and creator, to the living God, the only true all-embracing consciousness of life. Life and community can exist in God alone. He alone is the Spirit surrounding and connecting all things, for he is the love that rejoices in the self-sacrificing mutual relationship of all that lives. He alone is the power which is able to create new, unifying life, in the face of the severing power of death. Only in his love are we—hedged in and confined spirits as we are—able to rejoice in the whole and in its ultimate depths.

A HEALTHY INDIVIDUAL is one who sees with the eyes of love and acts in love. His conscious being

has been redeemed from its isolation and is
now turned to God. A sound, healthy person's
love goes out to all; he is no longer preoccu-
pied with himself. Instead, he puts himself into
the context of the whole, because he knows he
is placed there by the spirit of the whole. He
knows quite well that he himself is meant to
exist, but his life is not supplied from within
himself. He is called to be part of the life and
unfolding of the whole—of the totality of life—
his life is not grounded in himself but in the
creation and new creation of the whole. His life
consists only in the activity of the Spirit that
ceaselessly creates anew. The power of love and
life in this Spirit is the only power that makes
everything truly alive. So his affirmation of life
finds voice in different words than his previous
self-delusion did. Now the one ground for his
life and being is in the all-embracing life of the
Spirit who is the Word, the Word that conceives
and creates everything. Conscious of his smallness and limitation in the face of the greatness
of his calling, he can only say, "I am, for I am

being thought. I am alive, for I am being lived! I too have been created and called by the consciousness that penetrates all things, which includes me in itself and its activity." He finds his life in God's comprehensive oversight and penetration of the whole, in God's loving devotion to the whole.

A person who is on the way to health has to grasp the whole and live for the whole. He throws his own small, incapable self—which nonetheless has been called—into the great task of the comprehensive consciousness. He permits his own ego to flourish only insofar as it brings fruit and life for the whole.

TODAY ALL OF US are suffering from separation and isolation, lost in ourselves. Before we can attain the health and vitality of the only true life we must recognize the origin and the effect of our disease. Our thoughts are repeatedly bound up with ourselves; fundamentally we are able to see only our own point of view. We constantly call attention to ourselves; we fight for our own advantage, for our own little existence. We are sick and dying, diseased at the core. Our very life lies in death. We must diagnose our disease to be freed of it.

Whenever an organ forces itself on our attention it is unhealthy. The loud pumping of our heart when we climb, cycle, row, or ride tells us it is not in order. When we feel a stab of pain in our lungs, or worse still cough up blood; when our lungs make us keenly aware of their existence so that we have to concern ourselves with them—then it is clear that they are sick.

It is exactly the same with individual people in the community of mankind. When an individual makes himself noticeable, when he calls attention to himself, emphasizing and giving prominence to his own ego, it is obvious that he is sick. The vital context of healthy life is in deadly peril—endangered by himself. This is most clearly seen in hysterical and psychopathic cases, in neurasthenics or sufferers from weak nerves. We all know such people. Perhaps we are all like this?

We all know the unhealthy state of the nerves in which we (or others) try to impress those around us by making the most extraordinary remarks. If this does not succeed, we attempt to attract attention by witticisms and jokes. When this does not work either we drive people to notice us by angering them with our insolence. When even such measures fail, self-induced hysterics culminate in shivering, weeping, fainting, or even in genuine (or almost genuine) attempts at suicide. These succeed in forcing everyone, however unwilling, to pay attention to our diseased, isolated ego.

Because the diseased ego is no longer able to draw the attention of its fellows through talent or achievement, it soon takes to insolence and undisguised abnormality. The ego is sick as long as it lets its own little self come to the fore; it is sick as long as it is touchy and hypersensitive and always feels pushed into the background, as long as it continually wants to be treated differently, to be noticed more than is natural in the life of the whole. This disease is fatal: it is a sign of decomposition. This importunate obtrusiveness—this sickness, this crumbling decay and isolation—exposes the advanced dissolution of integrated life.

The sickness of the world lies in just this isolation of the accentuated ego and of every area of its activity. An individual who feels no one's pain but his own cannot identify with the world's suffering. He cares only for himself, fights only for his own existence, and ultimately seeks only his own improvement and happiness. He can neither feel the pain of others nor respond to the suffering of the world. Instead he increases the suffering. He has become a parasite dangerous to the whole. Such an individual has severed himself from life as a whole, from reality and the consciousness of unity that belongs to it. Cut off, he must finally perish, and his very death, being highly infectious, spreads death.

When we speak of the interdependence of life, we must talk first of all about joy: how the individual and the joy of conscious existence as a whole—the individual and joy in the life of all—belong together. For love that comes from the creative spirit of life is also joy. But let us not deceive ourselves. In our present society, world wide suffering actually demands a call for solidarity; it constitutes almost the only thing men share in practice.

Today, joy in life is no longer the common property of mankind. Today any joy we have in life is meager and stunted. The overwhelming majority of working people of our time are cut off from all access to the joy of life. They are cut off from every practical possibility of a really communal life. All that mankind has in common today is suffering. Joy is alive in this suffering only as hope, but nonetheless as joyful faith in a better future.

Without this joyful courage there would be no mutual help. The help given by one person to another proves that in spite of everything, faith in future healing cannot die. If a finger is hurt the whole body is involved, the whole body is drawn into active sympathy. It summons emergency squads in the bloodstream as soon as the nervous system has conveyed the message to the center of consciousness. A powerful and devoted defense force is called out to protect life. From all parts defenders rush to the place of attack; when one member suffers all members suffer with it.

This consciousness of unity—the soul of the body and the spirit of the human being—turns these subconscious processes into responsible actions for the health and efficiency of the body in the service of the spirit. In the whole animate world we meet the same active courage to intervene with joy and hope; me meet it in humankind as well, from man to man.

We recognize that it is deadly—the work of demons—when one member of the body withdraws from this devoted mutual service. It is demonic when an individual member breaks away from the rulership of the uniting soul and from the spirit that permeates the whole, when he insistently craves his own isolated, soulless, and unspiritual will.

This devilish work of setting the individual

adrift from the soul is at its most obvious in diseased sexuality. We encounter the same deviltry, however, in each individual egotistic will separated from the spirit of the whole. Today this demonic power rules personal and public life everywhere. Even some religious, patriotic, and social groups are dominated to a great degree by this demonic, self-centered spirit. All associations remain demonically soulless when consciously or unconsciously they emphasize their own exclusive goals and interests, when they act autonomously, acknowledging only their own laws, set up to meet their own egotistic demands. They have turned their backs on the living spirit of real community life in which each one gives himself wholly to serve the other.

These groups lack integration within the unifying soul that motivates the whole and lives in and for the whole. They estrange themselves completely from the spirit that leads to future unity, from the spirit which urges to union with the highest. They evade the creative, renewing power which constantly transforms dead and crumbling matter to coherent life. They lack the impulse and upsurge of the unity that belongs to true life. They lack the joyful dedication of love to all that is still alive, even in the midst of death. Only the powerful spirit of all-embracing love can deliver them from their self-willed separation and bring them to the unity of life. As individuals, as groups, or as mankind as a whole, we can be saved from the deadly disease of our age only if we break out of our individualistic isolation and turn to that fellowship in which the one Spirit welds all into one heart and one soul.

Today there is still no global society. There is still no community of mankind. Yet in the midst of those who are deeply divided and falling prey to death, among the many who are isolated and mutually hostile, there lives and works a hidden organism of the new creation. Mankind *is* one coherent body, because there is the one Spirit to give it consciousness.

We can see nothing of this hidden working of God, however, until we grasp the fact that our present condition, both public and personal, is one of most extreme and desperate need. We must become aware that the body of humanity is mortally sick. First it must become the greatest and most desperate distress for us that the need of the world consists in the deadly isolation of those who should have confronted it in solidarity and as one body. Only then can the mystery of the Church touch us.

Though the need seems to take on two aspects, it comes from one and the same disease: isolation as world suffering and world suffering as isolation. This is the only way we can understand the need of the world. When we individuals find a common bond in our suffering, then, and not till then, can we find the faith that it will be overcome. There would be no world need if there were no individuals who wanted to evade it instead of dedicating themselves completely to its relief. As long as there is need in the world, there is no single person who can free himself from it, no individual who is free from guilt for it.

OUR AGE IS IN THE PROCESS OF DYING; it is scorched with pain and need, and so there is a compulsion to absorb and conserve every drop of so-called life, however polluted. Like any dying man, we who belong to this age of decline feel driven to cling to our pain and intense suffering; life has left us nothing else to hold to. The goal of animate existence is not yet seen. Faith is still without its object; it is still unbelief.

The tortured poet of our age, therefore, knows neither the goal nor the God who faces him, waiting to grant him the future.[1] "My judge, I know nothing of the coming day. I do not know whether you will sit in judgment, my judge! Yet it is not your judgment day I fear, nor your almightiness, nor you yourself, my judge! I am afraid of myself; it is myself I fear, my own self. Whether you exist, my judge, I do not know. But, my judge, I long that you do exist!"

In spite of all his longing, man remains isolated in his tortured ego. He feels urged to bear

---

[1]The German Expressionist Franz Werfel (1890-1945) is quoted extensively in the following passages.

everyone's suffering with them, even feel the pain of death with them. The longing for love surges up everywhere. Yet people lack the power and the capacity for real love, for genuine, lasting love that entails action. "I am so blocked up! Everything yearns for love. I too weep for love; yet I like no one!" This "love" has no practical outcome. It remains unloving. Despite all the force and fervor of its expression, this "love" cannot rise above a sweet enjoyment of pain, a sympathy whose source is weakness.

Only when creative love is born out of our own pain; when our life is filled with the action that unity requires; when the conscience, quickened by God, is absolutely certain of fulfillment in deeds—only then can there be a response to the cries, "It ought not to be like that!" "That cannot be allowed!" In the freeing power of confident faith, the answer is given: "It will not stay like that! Life is stronger than death."

Yet we are still far from being certain that dawn is coming, because we have not actually experienced the darkness of night in its impenetrable

blackness. We have not known it in all its unfath-
omable suffering, even if in our imagination we
have "experienced the death of the whole world:
died with each outcast, with every alley cat and
old nag; rotted away as a dead soldier in the
desert; met our end as a convict."

Perhaps some of us may have felt this so personally that we can say, "I know the feelings of
the lonely women who play in hotel orchestras;
the trembling of actors near the prompter's box
as they make their debut. I have lived in the
woods, been a station master, sat bent over account books, served impatient guests. As a
stoker I have fed boilers whose flames scorched
my face; as a coolie I have eaten table scraps."

Perhaps we think that by feeling the suffering of others so keenly, we have been lifted out
of our isolation as individuals who once recognized nothing except "I exist." Perhaps we
know what it means to "be at one with the soul
of the universe . . . to feel the thousandfold
agony of the whole world's death in the tired
cab-horse, the drowning sailor, the starving

child of the factory hand."

Each one who is appalled and shaken by these feelings begins to sense dimly the will of the Spirit. But more is necessary than this feeling of fellowship with the universal spirit in its suffering—a spirit we would so much like to address. However, we cannot address it as "thou," but only as "we"—"I name thee, and say of everything, 'We are.'" To embrace without discrimination everything within this emotionally exciting "we" is still in the sphere of erotic longing. It is a desire to share in retrospect, and with pleasurable pain, all the experience of all creatures. It remains a longing born of our own insatiable thirst for life. The sympathy, boundless as it may be, is bent on satisfying a craving to extend the individual's own hold over life.

Primitive egotism still asserts: "I can do everything, everything!" But, still—"I will not sacrifice myself." The power of this avidly emotional ego will not be broken until we follow the way of sacrifice in practice. Even in our physical bodies we can live and thrive only through the continual sacrifice of living cells. There, too, the sacrificial death of individual cells is demanded to preserve and renew the life of the whole.

Millions are oppressed, languishing, barely alive. Millions "gasp, sweat, and kick under the burden of life and the fear of death." True identification with them can come only the hard way of personally sharing their need. We must expose ourselves to the all-too-real horrors of their daily life, together with those who are physically enervated, spiritually ruined, and emotionally diseased. We can comprehend the measureless suffering of the world and the unsolved need of man only when we ourselves actually suffer poverty, shame, and want. We can speak about them only when our words come from the very depth of our hearts.

When we dare to share in the suffering and life of those who are exposed to the most extreme want, we learn to understand what Schopenhauer means when he says, "Optimism is a truly wicked way of thinking; it mocks the unspeakable suffering of humanity."[2] If we are

[2]Arthur Schopenhauer (1788-1860), German philosopher.

living cheek by jowl with the unjust suffering of the masses, it becomes impossible to enjoy for ourselves alone the material goods of this world, the pleasures of life, or even the "justness of universal history."

All our present-day attempts to immerse ourselves in the morass of sympathy—as with our contemporary Franz Werfel, whose words we have been quoting—differ from a happy optimism only in their presenting the opposite side of the same coin. Pessimism too can become the self-indulgence of a sensitive soul full of concern for the world. Along this path we find no solution, not even to our own soul's anguish. All these efforts reveal only more deeply the insincerity of our feelings, our own torn and divided condition. We are again confronted with world need as the unredeemed drive for expansion of the individual ego.

The whole of human need is compacted into the unredeemed suffering of our own smallness. What torments the individual in the cosmos racks him above all else in his own being. What he finds so grievously missing in the world, he is bereft of in his own soul. So the vain surge of thinking and seeking—the hope to blend the ego into a boundless unity with the whole world—drains away.

Every barrier between the ego and the surrounding world must fall away because world need is individual suffering. And in actual fact, the world of dissension, the world of strife and hatred, the world of destruction and disunity is living unredeemed in each individual no less than in the larger world with its wars, class struggles, and economic rivalries.

The spirit that knows itself is therefore bound to fear itself. For this reason a man cries out to the Father in prayer, "Free me, cleanse me, my Father; kill this enemy, kill me, drown this 'me.'" He is forced to accuse himself; he passes judgment against himself with fanatic hatred: "They reproached me for being a sham, without character, vain, lazy, indifferent; too small to sin, too petty to do good, ineffectual in doing evil, a failure in the part assigned me. I heard them and took sides against myself and said: they are right—and I must hate myself."

Every man of today knows he is wretched; he is at cross purposes with himself, divided within himself. He sees the enemy within his own breast and loathes this other self that assaults him, squanders the treasure of his soul, devastates his conscience, and stifles his love. This enemy lures him to such base action that he has to cry out in his agony: "Why have you created me to this misery, my Father? Why have you given me a double nature? Why have you not given me unity and purity? Purify me, unify me, O waters! See, from the beginning of time, all your children who know themselves have wailed and lamented over this number, this two." It is the curse under which we suffer, two instead of one. Dividedness and isolation: there lies the world's need.

The overall misery of this world today is inextricably connected with the feeling of guilt in each individual for his own dividedness. The deadly weakness of sin as separation consumes the vital energy of love. The curse of half-heartedness and disunity stands in the way of decision and fulfillment. World suffering in public life is consonant with the sum of personal guilt.

The somber words of Schopenhauer force themselves on us: "If you want to know in moral terms the total worth of mankind, consider their common fate: want, misery, need, torment, and death. If, taken as a whole, they were not so worthless, then their general fate would not be so sad. If you could place all the torment on earth on one scale of a balance, and all the guilt of the world on the other, the indicator would certainly stand still."

The conflict between what should be and what is, the cleavage between man's direct calling and the inexorable fact of what he actually is, compels us repeatedly to ask: Where is life mortally wounded? What has poisoned life? Is there a poisonous root from which all suffering has sprung? Is there a poisonous spring of agony from which world need, like a mortal wound, is bound to bleed unstanched—unstanched, that is, if no help comes?

No ONE HAS FELT the suffering of mankind as Jesus did; it is he who has seen into its heart and exposed its root as no one else has. He knew human need as no other has. He knew the deepest root of need lies embedded in the divided heart, in the torn condition of man's deepest being. Jesus revealed the heart of man. He exposed the poison working there: separation and withdrawal, isolation and disintegration.

This blood-poisoning has gone so deep and has such a hold on mankind that it is impossible to measure the degree of individual guilt by the greatness of the suffering. On hearing the appalling news that under Pilate streams of human blood had been mingled with the blood-offering of slaughtered animals, Jesus said: "Do you think that these Galileans were worse sinners than all the others because they suffered this way? Or those eighteen who died when the tower in Siloam fell on them—do you think they were more guilty than all the others living in Jerusalem? I tell you, no! But unless you repent, you too will all perish."

The life of humankind—our relationship to each other—is so decayed, so fatally poisoned, that no legally convicted criminal can be more guilty than we are. In the final analysis we stand already condemned: the "innocent" victim is as guilty as the murderer. This recognition is the crucial step back toward life. We must recognize the "life" we live today, our whole life, as unjust and disintegrating into complete ruin—a personal injustice which at the same time is a public injustice. We must see *our* guilt in the mortal anguish of the whole world. This confession of both comprehensive and personal guilt is the ultimate, most crucial step we mortals can take.

This distress of conscience is the deepest, most crucial affliction. The indescribable agony that Luther experienced in his Black Tower could not be expressed in words. Unless we know what Luther suffered in his isolation and despair, we cannot grasp his faith. Only this agony under God's wrath and remoteness makes it possible to understand the certainty and joy of faith which was awakened in Luther as an entirely new experience. Luther wrote:

> I too know a man who declares he has often suffered this agony. True, it did not last long, but it was so intense and so hellish that no tongue can tell of its severity, no pen can describe it, nor can any man believe it who has not undergone it himself. If it had reached its peak or continued for half an hour longer—yes, for only a tenth of an hour longer—he would have been utterly destroyed and all his bones burned to ashes. Here God appears intensely angry, and all creation with him, so that man does not know where to turn. There is no comfort either from within or without; everything accuses him.

Luther felt intense hatred for this "just" God, whom he saw before him full of wrath and punishment, whose appeasement and fellowship he had striven for in vain. Today, many whose experience appears similar to Luther's, but whose consciousness of guilt is only shallow, consider the general and obvious judgment of God on humanity as "unjust."

Even if we are far from sharing the same personal distress over separation from God, or recognizing it as the result of our personal sin, we still share in the same sins as far as self-will is concerned, and in the same despair over our isolation.

WE NEED NOTHING BUT TRUTHFULNESS—an integrity that sees things as they really are—to recognize in every area of life our immense responsibility for the guilt of the whole. We need only look at tiny children among us to feel the overwhelming weight of our responsibility for the need and guilt caused by our overall isolation.

The child is lost in the midst of humanity; the child's garden has become an empty, desolate waste. This shows how deeply we have destroyed the unity of mankind. The earth has lost the paradise of God's unity because we have broken the living links uniting us to him.

If a person would adopt even a few children from conditions of physical and spiritual misery, he would be forced to face the unavoidable interrelationship of world need and individual guilt. The degeneracy of the child-world, starved of all relationships, stems from our sin, our egotistic focus on self-interest.

Nearly a quarter of the children of working women grow up practically motherless.[3] The mother is so weighed down with factory work, housework, and the care of her husband and children that the child cannot be led to a vital and fulfilled community life.

Mankind's sin inevitably imprints degeneracy on a child's very beginning. Born to heartlessly exploited, sick, worn-out parents, its pregnant or nursing mother mercilessly mistreated, the child suffers malnutrition even in the womb.

Such a child is deprived of health even as an

---

[3]Many of the statements in the following section are dated, and one or two statistics have been omitted. Essentially, however, they hold as true today as they did in Eberhard Arnold's time.

embryo; how can we hope to lead it to life and fellowship? Yet the child's life-potential is weakened at its very inception, not least by the general indifference to the strain and overwork inflicted on its mother during pregnancy. The harm is done not only in factories, where the mother's body is poisoned by tobacco and lead to the point of miscarriage. (Of the few pitiable children who reach birth despite these conditions, many die.)

The worst poisoning comes from other more hateful forms of social guilt—through blood diseases caused by unfaithfulness and promiscuous sexual relationships of unbridled lust. It is not unusual to see a gifted child, lively and agile, fall suddenly to the ground in spasms. The doctor makes a blood test. The innocent child has to suffer painful medical treatment, real torture, with the results still doubtful. The child's future is threatened by permanent defects like weak eyesight or severe mental aberration—the harvest of irresponsible nights.

A million illegitimate children are born in

our midst each year. The irresponsible, antisocial conduct of their fathers is visited on these children in the cruel practical disadvantages and social deprivation they suffer in life. Children abandoned by their parents are often severely harmed in their growing years by their foster mothers. And even if "mothers" avoid burdening their consciences with the slow, agonized death of their charges through backstreet abortions (it happens more often than we realize), they can rarely feel warm mother-love for the children, who are extremely difficult because they are so unhappy.

The fearful situation of these "superfluous" children would make the eyes of the hardest among us open and overflow. The worst self-reproach will well up in us that selfish individualism allowed us to pass over these monstrous facts for so long a time.

Every fifth child among us is born to die early. In the crowded loneliness of the city, bottle-feeding a baby is too often a slow poisoning because the infant formula nourishes death rather than life. Worse, there are accursed conditions in which the child is fed with alcohol instead of milk.

Epilepsy, idiocy, convulsions, mental deficiency, and psychopathic weakening of the senses and willpower are their fate to the third and fourth generation, chiefly because of alcohol and syphilis. They point to things that could be abolished today, or at least reduced to a minimum, if only men could rouse themselves to a common concern. No one who has seen the statistics of criminal and alcoholic families can deny any longer that through inheritance this two-fold contamination, vice and disease, has mushroomed into frightful world misery and need.

Even if here or there a little child manages to pass these first deadly reefs, most poor children are without homes in a sea of houses, homeless in their fatherland. Shut off from all air fit for human lungs, these unhappy beings dwell in their basements, attic cubicles, and shanties. In Germany today, thousands "live" with four or five others in one room, usually very small.

Except for those who have grown up in such quarters themselves, I am afraid only a very small number of us know about these conditions, let alone once visit them ourselves. That is the grave charge that must be raised against us: we have remained indifferent and insensitive to this world need at our very doorstep.

While we may work hard, we find time almost every day for some recreation and relaxation for ourselves. Isolated and egotistic as we are, we have no time to find the all-too-near places where we can come into heart-breaking contact with world need.

Imagine just one such "room." It is never large: a small room in which five people, day and night, have to survive. No one has a bed to himself. This is typical of the culture we are collectively responsible for: that several must always share a bed.

Breathe the foul air of this poorly heated little room in the cold of winter. Experience the moral dangers of this over-crowding, the early introduction of young children to hateful things that inevitably occur. Feel in our own bodies the inescapable, bacillus-infested filth of this poverty-stricken life in such a cramped space. Pen ourselves together with four exhausted, spent people in this narrow room, where sleeping space, sheets, and blankets are indescribably inadequate.

Imagine ten such rooms on one floor, and five such floors—fifty of these miserable torture-chambers. Imagine ten such buildings, five hundred such accursed "rooms." Then visualize these dens of human misery for five hundred thousand bodies in a thousand towns. In this way perhaps even the most hardened can grasp the misery in our Germany, where excessive numbers of opulent and luxurious houses are being built.

In this same Germany, a million people are homeless, people who for the most part have been unable for years to find employment or accommodation fit for any human being. Of course, in every housing office one can find a few skilled egotists who know how to pull the right strings to get an apartment in good time. But most are unfortunates who struggle in vain week after week, month after month, and year after year for decent housing. How many of them have children who because of these disgraceful conditions must grow up without the guidance of their parents, without home life!

We all know the Christmas Story about the child in the stable who could find no room among human beings. In our festively decked rooms we hang up pictures and set up beautifully lighted crib scenes with figures at the manger. We edify ourselves by trying to feel the poverty and need in which the Christ Child was born of his homeless mother—in a stable outside human habitation. And yet we allow countless children in our own "homeland," our "fatherland," to be without their own little beds! Why do we not go to these children who have not even a stable to shelter them from storm and rain? That would not be the worst home for many who are driven from pillar to post in our day.

Many an unfortunate mother contemplates suicide for the sake of her child. Only as an orphan has her child any prospect of having a bed—in an institution.

Children who are diagnosed as psychopathic, too, and children who have been placed under supervision because of their parents' misconduct, are cared for by the State through youth welfare centers and case workers. We have to be thankful for this social initiative which is securely established in the State: it is a sign of mounting need and also of an awakened sense of social responsibility. We acknowledge unreservedly this activity of the State, whose most effective way of combating the evils of society is through its "good works."

The State, however, is based on property and militarism, assuming the legal use of force as a necessity: it is outside of Christianity. We can pay State taxes and receive social welfare support from it only as long as neither endangers our life of faith, love, and expectation of the kingdom of God.

State welfare has its limitations. It must be supplemented by the help of individuals and private volunteer organizations. There are so many, many children in extreme need who are not under the care of the State because they are neither psychopathic nor victims of child abuse. For these there is usually no possibility of State support in money or social care.

It is these marginal cases who need our special attention. Here it is important to explore the need and examine conditions as exactly as possible. Only as we take this world need upon our own shoulders through constant investigation shall we be able to recognize its weight and bear our small share of it.

Look into children's lives as you meet them. Look into the pain countless mothers bear for their children in mortally wounded hearts. Cut back your own requirements to the utmost and take children into your own home. When your accommodations are stretched to the limit, as full as healthy housing permits, contact children's homes where children are brought up in a spirit of trust and joy, where there is attentive care and children are led to develop their best potential.

The need of the world is revealed in children. Needy children grow up dwarfed and stunted. What a contrast there is between such a tiny, undergrown creature and a normally-developed child of the same age! If we read the reports of school doctors from the time following the World War, we are appalled by the emaciation and resulting deaths among children, by the overall physical deterioration, and especially by the widespread tuberculosis that the figures reveal.

It has been impossible to find out how many starving children in a large city go to school without breakfast. It would be an enormous figure. The best school can accomplish nothing when faced with the intellectual void of hungry children. The barbarous exploitation of child labor—fought against by all socialists—and even the cruel thrashing of children by parents who are at the end of their tether are much more closely correlated with the torturous battle against hunger than anyone wants to admit.

The gravest guilt of human society is starkly revealed by the thousand paths that lead from this abysmal need to the filthiest depravity and crime.

Prostitution—selling young bodies for wretched money—is an extreme symptom of poverty. Prostitution increases in direct proportion to the degree of unemployment and low wages. In the same way the number of illegitimate births parallels the fall and rise of poverty. There is an inseparable link between poverty and degradation. On the streets or in brothels the daughters of the poor are doomed to go under.

Everyone should hear, just once, how these unfortunates curse their existence, should see them grovel before mere human beings in a welfare home, see them die slowly in a hospital or take their own lives. Once, just once, we should witness the depths to which our apathy and indifference have brought these children of need.

"Corruption greets one everywhere in these offspring of long, dark alleys—loveless and without God. The way is gruesome. The whole world is sad to the point of despair."

All these dark rays which reach us from the world of need—so near, and yet so far—signal distress and cry out for light to illumine the darkness. Cry upon cry falls on ears reluctant to acknowledge the relationship of misery to our heavy share in the guilt that arises from our whole way of life. They compel us to take to heart the need of the world and to locate its source in our apathetic isolation.

Wretched housing conditions—the product of greed—are a chief source of this misery. The way capitalists treat their employees when there is a work-related accident reveals our commonest form of injustice and inconsistency: the disparity between work and wages, between work on the one hand and the lack of protection for the worker on the other.

To take these questions seriously requires dedicated effort—not only research into reliable source material, but more important, getting to know social workers and living and working with them. We must hunt out the areas of need and misery with them. We must open our hearts and doors to all who are destitute in order to feel our common experience, our common need, and our common responsibility.

TODAY'S NEED CONFRONTS US with the fate brought upon the world and humanity, the nemesis of guilt. All of us are involved; it is not a matter of exceptions and unusual cases. The most frightening aspect of this fate that hangs over humanity is its inescapability. No one can escape by running away. The very inevitability of disaster and guilt adds that last intensification of suffering which makes it so terrible a distress. The futility of attempts to relieve this misery, the disillusionment that is bound to follow human efforts to overcome it, lead to the verge of a despair worse even than a revulsion for life.

We seemed to have almost forgotten our rejection of life and contempt for humanity, with all the enervating weariness and wild despair that attended them. But now they surface again.

This shows us how far we were from overcoming them. Today not a few find their noblest expectations disappointed. They are utterly disheartened, because their most sacred hopes are betrayed and subverted. They do not yet see that this disillusion liberates them from false expectations and creates room for that real faith without which all hope is a hollow lie.

We are far from that faith today. Doubt seems to swallow up all hope; everything is doubted: the will and capacity of mankind today, the history of the universe and the ultimate future of humanity. Still worse, there is doubt and uncertainty about the purpose of our destiny. Many give up all hope in the Spirit, because everywhere they see only what is demonic; only madness, selfishness, and betrayal.

This gnawing doubt about all that is good in man, about the destiny and goal of our existence, works its way to the depths of our being, bringing us to the brink of absolute despair. Despair is the last hell into which we can sink. It shatters every capacity for faith; it ends all hope.

It shuts out love; it makes it impossible to continue living. Despair is death in utter devastation and dissolution.

In this despair, our fate will be like that of Prometheus. According to the oldest myth, his agony consisted in having his flesh torn apart ever anew under a searing sun. But it remained bodily pain only, purely physical torture.

Prometheus had brought fire to the human race, hoping to raise it out of the misery of its animal existence. For this he has to suffer, helpless and unarmed, as day by day the vultures of Zeus tear at his liver—precisely his liver—consuming just enough to perpetuate this incessant bodily torment through all eternity. The heart is in this position when the need of the world daily tears our innermost being—and from time immemorial the liver has symbolized this anguish. The poet Aeschylus understood the age-old form of the myth in a deeper sense, involving the soul. He transplanted Prometheus's suffering to the innermost depths of life as spiritual anguish. The fire-bringer had intervened on humankind's behalf, throwing himself into a titanic struggle with the deity. Now he had to undergo the worst suffering possible for him to endure.

In despair, Prometheus had to learn that for him the very being of the deity had become envy and injustice. For him, all that happens in the world is nothing but catastrophe, blood, and filth. The godhead whom he was supposed to honor has become for him an egotistic, satanic being. Now the god wants to destroy the fire-bringer who as half-god, half-man dared to bring "good" to men without his permission.

So Prometheus hangs chained to the rock, angry, rebellious, and full of hatred. As the vultures tear at his liver, his torment has become the utmost anguish of spirit. It is this godforsakenness, this hostility of the deity that tortures him with the despairing thought that there may be no god who works for good. How could such universal anguish, such malevolent injustice, be imposed on mankind otherwise?

Where man despairs, there is no God; when we despair, we despair of God. But when we despair of God, we despair of everything—of people, of mankind, of life. Prometheus had to despair. He lacked the all-revealing insight that no cultural progress is able to help torn humanity—only God can help, the God of life and love whom men have lost.

God alone—instead of giving seductive, perishable, treacherous gifts—can and will create again what had been lost. He gives us back the possibility of life. Prometheus had to despair, for he was unable to recognize the unifying, light-giving spirit of creative goodness and its final battle with the dark, dividing, destroying powers of fire.

Despair is just as much a question of God as faith is. Sin is revealed as separation, ultimately separation from God; it is dissociation from God, who is the source and oneness of life. As Jesus perceived it, falling away from God is the root of misery.

The distress of conscience suffered by Luther is the fear that a righteous but wrathful God will drive the sinner far from his presence. Faith believes in God as the spirit of unity. For this reason, and for this reason alone, it is faith for man, faith in the calling God has given him. Despair is isolation, a severed connection, a broken relationship, the opposite of faith. Faith is trust and uniting, a triumphant trust in unity that overcomes all barriers.

Only faith is capable of bearing world need, because faith knows the one who unites, who is greater than all separation and division. Only love that comes from faith is able to draw strength out of suffering, strength to overcome. Only love, through its absolute acceptance of every suffering, can give the impetus for the utmost activity and new fulfillment. Just as there is no faith without God, there is no love without faith.

There are always men who despair, for we are threatened on all sides by a darkening of the divine light. Despair lies latent in us all, because in all of us the Adversary is at work, pitting human fire—with the lying, divisive might of cultural progress and its devilish terms for existence— against the misery and torment of the present world order.

Yet there are people everywhere who have faith, because the eternal light of God's unifying goodness overpowers all darkness and cannot be consumed by it. Faith is latent in everyone, for the revelation of creative light illumines every man who enters this dark world.

FAITH CAN SPRING only from the very darkest point in the darkness of this world. He who went through the deepest suffering of the world was, like Prometheus, bound fast. But while Prometheus was fettered by his chains to a life of eternal captivity, this other, Jesus, was brought by the nails that pierced him to a death that liberates and unites. Whereas Prometheus had kindled the hearth-fire of human culture, this Other brought the completely different fire of revelation and uniting to the earth—the love of God.

Yet he, just he, was the one who had to call out in the most extreme anguish of soul, "My God, my God, why hast thou forsaken me?" With his believing, uniting spirit, his suffering on the cross went deeper than all the suffering of human despair. We are not speaking here of the physical agonies of a bloody execution, although the reality and consequences of his death had the most profound significance. Christ's torture was not like that of Prometheus, a half-human doubt about the goodness and power of God. But it was the reality of his death as separation from God, from the sole secret of life—and above all *his* life—which plunged Jesus into the final agonies of extreme need.

In this spiritual night of utter forsakenness Jesus sank to the deepest depths of world need. And in the boundless isolation of death, he became victor over the world's need because he suffered it at its worst. Had he not endured it to the full, he would not have had the power to overcome it.

Now he could pray for his enemies. Now he could cry out, "It is finished!" The victory of the God of light and his revelation of the ultimate uniting of life was won in the only decisive place the battle could be fought—in the darkest death. So, on account of this one decisive point, there exists—in the midst of the fear and misery of the world, in the most extreme suffering of complete abandonment by God—a last chance to believe. Out of the most deadly suffering rises the victory of resurrection. Only in this ghastly death does the resurrection draw near. Only upon this annihilation of loving life can the newness and unity of the coming God-given life be built.

That is the mysterious paradox of the execution outside Jerusalem: death was suffered in its greatest horror and was overcome for exactly that reason. Jesus died because of the world's need. And because of that, he lives—to overcome it. We do not live, for we are unwilling to die. We do not overcome the need, because we avoid its deepest horrors.

Whereas Prometheus could not die and therefore never reached the consummation of his torture—whereas he was left hanging forever in his despair—Jesus, in his death, completed his work through dying in complete godforsakenness. As the liberated and living one, as the liberating bringer of life, he could leave the gallows and the grave behind him. Condemned and crucified, pierced and dying, he could bring his work of union to perfection.

He united his mother and friend; he received the criminal into his fellowship; he united himself with his enemies by forgiving them; he gave up his spirit into the uniting spirit of his Father, that he might unite all his children. Through the breaking of his own body, he created the new organism of God's unity, the mystical body of the messianic Church.

The body of the coming Christ, mutilated on the gallows and there—precisely there—created anew, is the only true unity of God in this torn humanity. The dark tragedy of his death throes marks the beginning of the greatness of his light. In this way he became the one leader for all people, leading them into the deepest suffering of world need and out of its annihilating flame.

Every all-out battle for universal justice and love leads to death, just as Jesus died. World need is close to the Cross; here the suffering of the whole world is gathered. Here everything that otherwise collapses, scatters, and disappears is concentrated to the point of decision. The One who is all-powerful died to this life and became completely one with the whole of the world's suffering, so that once and for all it could be brought together, grappled with, and overcome. In this infamous execution, the suffering that embraced the very utmost of all need was transformed to love in action, which liberates and unites.

Jesus stripped himself of all his own rights and possibilities for power in order to suffer the worst, to be robbed of what he most treasured, without resisting. He did not seek death because he loved or desired it. Jesus wanted life. He wanted life in its true sense, as unity which overcomes dualism, separation, and disintegration. Just for this reason he wanted life for all those tortured by separation and isolation, for those who suffer the depths of misery, for the poor, the sinners, the guilty, and the despairing.

The battle in the spirit-world was decisive; the seemingly passive lack of resistance perfected a work which asserted the will of love and unity against all the opposition of hatred and division. Here the decision fell which frees the earth from the tyranny of discord and disintegration. The whole of suffering is concentrated here for its ultimate solution. The destiny of life is revealed in this death. Here God confronts humanity in its deadly laceration and strife.

The world with all its injustice—and in spite of its disunity—combines the powers of state, church, and nation to expel the One who alone and wholeheartedly lived for the goodness of God, the unity of all in all. So we see that while in this world of blatant injustice the good goes under, yet in that going under the original and ultimate purpose of this world, the Word who is God, is victorious.

Love is murdered; but love is stronger than death. So world history becomes world judgment, but in just this sense: that world history itself is judged and found to be unjust, and God nevertheless reveals himself in it as the only good and powerful one.

The great "antichrist" of our times has unintentionally characterized the need revealed and solved here, this last and deepest guilt of our world: "Man cannot suffer such a witness to live. . . . Once, men sacrificed human beings to their gods. The supreme sacrifice, however, is to sacrifice God himself. . . To sacrifice God—for nothing!. . . Where is God? We have killed him. We are all his murderers. The holiest and mightiest that the world has ever possessed is bleeding beneath our knives. Who will cleanse us of this blood?"[4]

HIDDEN BEHIND THE NEED of the world and our collective guilt lurks the beast of prey from the abyss: the sin of transgressing God. The death of Jesus makes it obvious that the world's need is ultimately its guilt. Only at the very pinnacle of the world's utmost wickedness could this guilt and need be overcome. The deepest source of all suffering is exposed: "Living without love and

---

[4] Here and in the next paragraph, Eberhard Arnold quotes Friedrich Nietzsche (1844-1900).

without God. . . . Nothing is lost—except the soul itself which has lost its God."

This crowning fact, the enormity of this loss, impels us to raise the crucial question: is God irretrievably lost? Or is God closer to us than ever, now that we realize we have lost him and cannot possibly bring back what is lost? Is he closer than ever, because we now know that he is the antithesis of our being and our lives?

We human beings have killed God. Now it is clear that true religion does not come from men; it is clear that human religion is without God. Now it must be seen whether God will turn his heart away from these murderers, who in their frenzied wickedness lacerate each other and him, their God; or whether he will reveal himself to them as the perfectly good One in this very hour of their extreme need and guilt.

Here the miracle of creative power begins. Here the Spirit of perfect love, the Spirit that creates life, can reveal himself. As never before, the Risen One brings to men God's nearness, his life that makes all things new. Jesus paves the new way for God to enter the world. This new way seeks out darkness but does not fall prey to it. Not until now can God in the out-pouring of his Spirit, unfold his heart to men in full forgiveness and reconciliation.

Now, to all who see him, God becomes bright and clear; for the contrast between his love and the oneness of his life on the one hand, and our world on the other, is revealed. Jesus had to die, because in a world ruled by Mammon, in the domain of impure spirits, among a murderous, lying, hypocritical mankind, he went the way of God, the way of life and the Spirit, the way of love and strength. This radiant way leads out-ward from his grave to meet the future!

God has come close to us. Jesus' way of death is God's way to Christ's resurrection. Who would fight the same fight must be ready, as he was, to be suppressed, wiped out, persecuted—killed. Anguish is piled upon anguish. If we wish to put into action what the infinite Spirit wills for this oppressed material world, if we believe that the earth, the land—everything—is intended for God and his Spirit alone, we have to become one with the God of a thousandfold agonies.

This means draining the cup of bitterness to its dregs. It means suffering death with God.

To dedicate this body and this earth to God means death, actual bodily death, ugly and earthly. For "life" is unjust; it will not tolerate justice. As soon as the spirit of assistance, the will to love, and its resulting community attempt to transform matter, to transform everything physical and material, the opposing spiritual power rears up with its entire murderous violence. Whoever attacks injustice must die.

What counts now—once the way and the goal are clear—is to sacrifice all one is and has. All "martyrdom," however agonizing it may be, amounts to nothing unless it has this goal and stays on this track. The only true martyrs are those who give witness. Thousands have been hanged and crucified. Yet Jesus alone could die a death out of which new life arose. It is only in Jesus that death leads to life. Suffering and death as such are merely an end, an abyss.

Christ alone is the risen one, who reveals that the living God is the power that brings an awakening out of death. The tidings of the man hung on the cross, of the end of Jesus' life, is inseparable from the fact of the resurrection, the new beginning of the coming Christ. The Christ who is present, who is the Spirit, bears all the suffering that his heart embraced in his death. He brings all power, manifest in the mystery of his resurrection, to perfect the unity of life which is of God.

ANYONE WHO GRASPS THIS FACT cannot be held in death through despair in God, for he has experienced the culmination of despair—its conquest through faith. Christ within us is the certain expectation that all things shall be unified and perfected in radiant love—that God lives and is coming! Even if we find no people anywhere who exemplify the way God lives and works in the spirit of pure love, still Jesus is and remains the love that is transformed into deed and reality: the liberation and redemption of mankind from all its suffering and guilt—the revelation of God.

If for one single time in history perfect love has become deed, has become flesh, then community with this first Son of a new humanity is our surety that the life of unity can and must become reality. No one need despair of love, no one need despair of God. Love has appeared; God is tangibly near!

In the crucified Christ and his rising to life, in the outpouring of his Spirit, and in his future, God comes to men—so that with him they suffer the death of evil and the collapse of human society today and find faith in forgiveness, resurrection, and unity—faith in God.

In Christ, God's ultimate future is revealed; a future in which the deeply divided body of humankind, that bleeds from every wound, shall be brought together as one organism, a living and inspired, spirit-filled unity of all its cells.

Earlier we allowed ourselves to envision the whole globe as inhabited by countless living beings, separate, yet so mutually related that all could compose the unified life of earth's cosmic totality, united, borne, and directed by one Soul and one Spirit. This vision will be realized. It is God's future for the earth. It shall be peopled by a unified humanity. There shall no longer be any isolated individuals, because all men shall live in a harmonious relationship under the rule of one Spirit only, God himself.

This unity, which results from a new act of creation, will show its reality in the mutual service of common work, in the solidarity of life on this planet earth. This earth and the people belonging to it will be one great whole in the unity of the Spirit who is to come. Death is overcome, decay and isolation have no more power.

Alive from the dead, this new-made life creates unity among all those who have the spirit of unity. Life in unity is eternal life; it does not pass away, for it embraces all people and all things. As a decisive, historic parable from God, it shall shine out upon the earth in a humanity made new, set free, and united.

EPILOGUE

Though little known today, Eberhard Arnold
(1883 –1935) was widely sought-after during his
lifetime as a public speaker, writer, lecturer, and
publisher in his native Germany. During and
after his studies at Breslau, Halle, and Erlangen
(from which he received his doctorate in 1909)
he was active in the student revival movement
then sweeping those towns and became secre-
tary of the German Christian Student Union. In
1916 he became literary director of the Furche
Publishing House in Berlin and editor of its
monthly.

Like thousands of young Germans in the
1920s, Eberhard and his wife Emmy were
disillusioned by the failure of the establish-
ment–especially the churches–to provide answers for the problems of society in the turbulent
years following World War I. In their seeking,
the Arnolds were influenced by the German
Youth Movement (in which Eberhard was a
nationally-known participant), the sixteenth-

century Anabaptists, the German pastor Johann Christoph Blumhardt and his son Christoph Friedrich, and most significantly, the early Christians.

In 1920, out of a burning desire to practice the clear demands in the Sermon on the Mount, the Arnolds with their five children and a few others began a communal life in the Hessian village of Sannerz. The community, which supported itself by agriculture and a small but vibrant publishing house, attracted thousands of visitors and grew quickly. By 1926 the house in Sannerz had become too small, and the next year a new *Bruderhof* ("place of brothers") was started in the nearby Rhön hills.

The 1930s brought persecution by the National Socialist regime and expulsion from Germany. After a temporary stay in neighboring Liechtenstein, the Bruderhof fled to England where a new Bruderhof–the Cotswold–was established. Here the first major undertaking of the publishing house was the translation of *The Individual and World Need*, whose appearance in 1938 attracted more than a few new English members. World War II drove the Bruderhof to Paraguay in 1940-41, and in the 1950s new Bruderhofs in New York, Connecticut, and Pennsylvania were established.

For all of us at the Bruderhof, the full community in which we live provides us daily with the opportunity to give ourselves in service to others for the cause of true brotherhood. It is no utopian escape. We–as all humans–face a fragment of world need in ourselves and in our neighbors and strive for answers to it. We are not, however, under the illusion that men, women, and children can live together in this world today in such a way as to escape its need and sickness, for the "world" situation is everywhere "our" situation, whether we live in full community or try to drop out of society, whether we live in the inner city or the rural hinterland or belong to the "normal" suburban mainstream.

Moreover, we are very well aware of our own human weakness as individuals and as a community. But we believe that discipleship of Jesus is a clear way of love, of freedom, and of truth in deeds and that we can be given the strength again and again to strive for it and to follow it freely and wholeheartedly. We seek fresh courage, hope, and faith to live in truer unity and brotherhood, wishing that the living spirit of the early Christians may constantly touch our lives, and the lives of all men and women anew.

With Eberhard Arnold we affirm: "This planet, the earth, must be conquered for a new kingdom, for a new order, for a new unity, for a new joy. This joy must come to us from the God who is the God of love, who is the Spirit of peace and of unity and community. That is the message Jesus brings. And Jesus had the faith and the certainty that this message can be believed today."

The editors

Seeking for the Kingdom of God: Origins of the Bruderhof Communities, by Eberhard and Emmy Arnold, 308 pages

Eberhard Arnold: A Testimony of Church Community from His Life and Writings, 120 pages

Living Churches: The Essence of Their Life

>   *Vol. 1 Love to Christ and Love to the Brothers,* 36 pages
>   *Vol. 2 The Meaning and Power of Prayer Life,* 64 pages

When the Time Was Fulfilled: On Advent and Christmas, by Eberhard Arnold, Emmy Arnold, Christoph Blumhardt, and Alfred Delp, 256 pages

The Early Christians after the Death of the Apostles, edited by Eberhard Arnold, 484 pages

The Early Anabaptists, 64 pages

Love and Marrage in the Spirit, 260 pages

Children's Education in Community, 68 pages

COMPLETE LISTING OF PLOUGH BOOKS
SENT ON REQUEST

For more infomation about the Bruderhof, write one of the communities listed below. Visitors are welcome.

Addresses of the current (1993) Bruderhofs of the Hutterian Brethren:

Catskill, Elka Park, NY 12427
Deer Spring, Norfolk, CT 06058
New Meadow Run, Farmington, PA 15437
Pleasant View, Ulster Park, NY 12487
Spring Valley, Farmington, PA 15437
Woodcrest, Rifton, NY 12471
Darvell, Robertsbridge, E. Sussex,
    TN32 5DR, ENGLAND
Michaelshof, W-5231 Birnbach, GERMANY
Palmgrove Center, P.O. Box 455, Utu-Abak
    Abak/Aks, NIGERIA